Learn to Swim the Australian Way
Level 4 Advanced
Written by AlyT

Learn To Swim the Australian Way
Level 4 Advanced

Part of the Learn to Swim the Australian Way series with AlyT

DEDICATED TO

my mother **RHONDA** aka **MRS PAUL**
who taught me everything I needed to know
about life & Jesus †

AND my mentor **PETER TIBBS** aka **TIBBSIE**; both
of whom helped mould me into the swimmer and
swimming teacher I am today.

Written by AlyT
© Copyright 2023 by Allison Tyson
All rights reserved. No part of this book may be used or reproduced in any manner whatsoever, including photocopying, social media platforms and/or other electronic or mechanical methods, without written permission of the publisher.
For more information write: Aly T, PO Box 6699, Cairns City, QLD 4870.

Illustrator: PicassoJR
Formatting: Aluycia Suceng
Editing: Phoenix Raig
First printing: 2023

Disclaimer
While we draw on our own prior professional expertise and background in the area of teaching learn to swim, by purchasing and reading our products you acknowledge that we have produced this book for informational and educational purposes only. You alone are solely responsible, and take full responsibility for your own wellbeing as well as the health, lives and wellbeing of your family and children in your care.

www.borntoswim.com.au
SwimMechanics@yahoo.com

Other books by this Author include:
Water Awareness Newborns
Water Awareness Babies
Water Awareness Toddlers
Learn to Swim the Australian Way Level 1 – The Foundations
Learn to Swim the Australian Way Level 2 – The Basics
Learn to Swim the Australian Way Level 3 – Intermediate

SAFETY FIRST!

* NEVER SWIM ALONE

Regardless of swimming ability, swimmers should ALWAYS be monitored by a responsible adult who can swim. Even good swimmers can drown.
Where possible, let the lifeguard on duty know you are learning to swim or a beginner swimmer.

* NEVER FORCE A SWIMMER UNDER THE WATER

Learning to swim should be fun & appropriate to the individual's pace. Be mindful of how you hold and help a swimmer as they learn; repeat cues and demonstrate skills as much as you can, and never use force.

* NEVER HOLD YOUR BREATH FOR EXTENDED PERIODS OF TIME

Hyperventilating and breath holding games are dangerous and can cause you to faint (lose consciousness) in the water (search shallow water black-out). Exchanging CO_2 and Oxygen via blowing bubbles is extremely important when swimming to avoid fatigue and to help the swimmer stay balanced.

* LEARNING TO SWIM IN SHALLOW, WAIST DEPTH WATER IS BEST FOR BEGINNERS

Until a swimmer can confidently move through the water and float comfortably on their back, beginner swimmers should continue to practise in shallow water.

A NOTE TO ALL OUR SWIM BUDDIES LEARNING TO SWIM,

CONGRATULATIONS on completing all the skills from our previous Learn to Swim levels. You've **LEARNT THE FOUNDATIONS** for good swimming and **THE BASIC SKILLS** for each of the strokes, dives, and so much more. Most importantly, you've learnt **HOW TO BE SAFER AND MORE CONFIDENT AROUND WATER**. Are you ready to complete your Learn to Swim journey?

Just as in our previous books, in level 4 we'll use 21 **NEW SKILLS** to help **BUILD MUSCLE MEMORY, IMPROVE BALANCE AND INCREASE TRACTION & PROPULSION** in the water. It's time to **PUT EACH PIECE OF THE LEARNING TO SWIM PUZZLE TOGETHER** and move on to the new challenge of **MASTERING EACH OF THE FOUR COMPETITIVE STROKES** (Butterfly, Backstroke, Breaststroke and Freestyle), our dives, starts and turns. We'll also learn **MORE FUN WATER-SAFETY STUFF** and how to **ADD SPEED, DISTANCE AND POWER** to our swimming.

FOR THE PARENTS AND TEACHERS who will be assisting with these skills, ensure your swimmer student **REHEARSES EACH SKILL CORRECTLY** (4-5 times every lesson) **UNTIL IT IS MASTERED**. Combining a poorly executed skill with a more complicated skill will confuse swimmers and lead to sloppy swimming. **DON'T** be afraid to **CORRECT MISTAKES, REVISE OLDER SKILLS** and **USE LOTS OF VERBAL & VISUAL CUES** before progressing to more complex skills. And remember always **GIVE LOTS OF PRAISE AND ENCOURAGEMENT**.

FOR OUR STUDENT SWIMMERS, remember that 'I can't' doesn't exist in the learner swimmer's vocabulary, but **'I'LL TRY' AND A BIT OF EFFORT** always should. Some skills you'll learn in minutes, others may take weeks or months of hard work. **TO FAST-TRACK LEARNING**, we encourage swimmers to **SLOW DOWN AND SHORTEN THE DISTANCE** they swim to 3-5 meters; practising and **REFINING EACH SKILL LITTLE BY LITTLE AT EACH LESSON**, at least three times a week and **PAYING ATTENTION TO THE SMALL DETAILS**. This will help **IMBED THE CORRECT MOTOR PATTERNS** and **ACCELERATE YOUR LEARNING**.

As always, our aim is to **TEACH EACH OF THE SKILLS IN THE RIGHT ORDER.** This allows our swimmers to **GRADUALLY PROGRESS** in a way that **DEVELOPMENTALLY MAKES SENSE**, allowing them to achieve **THE DESIRED RESULTS IN THE SHORTEST AMOUNT OF TIME**; incorrect practise of a poorly executed skill will only reinforce bad technique and make the swimmer slower, less efficient in the water and take longer to learn to swim.

Once again, for ease of learning, we've included **VISUAL CUES, CATCHY NAMES** and easy-to-remember **VERBAL CUES** for each of the skills. All learner swimmers, teachers and parents should follow the motto **'LEARN SLOW TO SWIM FAST'**, and adhere to the four P's of learning: **PATIENCE, PRAISE, PERFECTION AND PRACTICE**.

Yours swimmingly,

PS The **EASIER WE MAKE IT** for swimmers to move through the water, the **SOONER AND FASTER** they will swim.
ALL THE SMALL DETAILS COUNT.

I CAN DO A STEP-IN & PUSH-OUT ENTRY!

I do a Step-In entry when I am entering shallow water.

Before jumping into the water, I first check:
1. the depth of the water?
2. is there a safe place for me to get in and out of the water?
3. is someone close by paying attention, watching to help me if I need them?

Elbows up

After finding a safe place to enter, I stand on the edge of the pool and step off into the water. I keep my knees slightly bent, ready to absorb the impact as I hit the floor of the pool with my feet.

I practise my Push-Outs to exit the pool. A Push-Out helps strengthen the muscles in my chest, arms and back.

To Push-Out of the water, I bring myself close to the pool wall and place my hands flat, under my armpits, on the pool deck. I lift my elbows up high as I lean forward and press down firmly with my hands to drive myself up and out.
If I am Pushing-Out of deep water, I count to 3, jump upwards and kick downwards with both my feet, as I push down with my hands.

When I have lifted myself high enough, I turn and sit on the side or climb the rest of the way out using my legs and feet.

I CAN BELLY BREATHE & SINK DOWN!

Belly Breaths and Sink Downs help me to train my breath. I float better and swim further if I stay in control of my breathing.

Belly Breathing teaches me to relax and breathe deeply. I Belly Breathe by standing up straight and placing my hands on my belly just under my ribs. I take in a quick, deep breath and let it out long and slow through my nose and mouth. I feel my hands rise and fall as I breathe in and blow out.

After practising a few standing Belly Breaths, I do a couple of Sink Downs to teach myself to exhale long and slow under the water. I Sink Down and blow bubbles out through my nose and mouth as I count to 5.

When I run out of breath, I return to the surface, take in another Belly Breath and sink back down again.

BREATH IN!

BREATH OUT!

1. 2. 3. 4. 5!

After I do this 5 or 6 times, I feel relaxed and ready to swim.

I CAN POWER TRIANGLES

BUTTERFLY

BACKSTROKE

POWER TRIANGLES

BREASTSTROKE

FREESTYLE

There are 5 phases to the arm cycle for each of the competitive strokes:

1 THE ENTRY
my hand enters the water and my arm extends forward

2 THE CATCH
my hand tilts slightly downwards and grabs onto the water

3 THE PULL
my arm bends, and I pull myself through the water keeping the pressure of the water on my hand

4 THE PUSH
my hand pushes the water to my hip (or to my chest for Breaststroke) and finishes moving under the water

5 THE RECOVERY
my arm travels over the surface of the water to start the cycle again.

I use Power Triangles during the Pull phase as I swim. Power Triangles make me a stronger swimmer, allowing me to swim faster and further.

I make a Power Triangle by bending my arm at the elbow while keeping my wrist and hand firm. The length from my fingertips to my elbow acts as a paddle to help move me through the water as I swim.

I CAN HYPERSTREAMLINE

I add a Hyperstreamline to my Torpedo Streamlines and Swordfish Starts to maximise speed as I dive into the water or take off from the wall.

Arms behind ears

Chin to chest

STRETCH

SQUEEZE!

A tight Hyperstreamline keeps my body flat and narrow, reducing drag as I cut through the water like an arrow. Drag is the water pushing against you, slowing you down. It makes moving through the water harder than it needs to be.

To practise my Hyperstreamline, I Torpedo Stretch on the pool deck or in shallow water. I start by placing one hand over the other and locking them together with my thumbs. Then I stretch my arms up over my head, keeping them behind my ears, and squeezing my elbows against the back of my head. As I squeeze and stretch upwards I look straight ahead and keep my chin tucked against my chest.

I learn to Belly Breathe and balance in this position before crouching and jumping as high as I can.

When I am ready, I practise a Swordfish Start from the side of the pool and Hyperstreamline my Torpedo through the water, releasing a stream of bubbles onto my chest as I kick three fast Body Dolphins to get myself back to the surface.

I CAN DO A MISSILE START!

1. I practise my Missile Start by standing on the pool deck or in shallow water, looking straight ahead and resting my hands, palms down, on my thighs.

2. Before I begin, I take in a deep Belly Breath and as I exhale I bend my elbows so my fingertips almost touch. I then slide my hands up the center of my body, past my chest and face, and reach my arms up over my head.

3. Once my hands have passed my face, I turn them over so my palms are facing outwards and my thumbs almost touch.

4. I keep my arms straight, squeezed against the back of my head, as I stretch in this position and take in another deep Belly Breathe.

I can also practise my Missile Starts in the water. I do this by Blasting Off with my arms by my sides, chin tucked against my chest and eyes looking straight down. As I do one slow Body Dolphin under the water, I bend my elbows until my fingertips touch and begin to draw my hands up as close to my body as I can – past my chest and my face. As my arms reach forward, my hands roll over, palms down, into a Missile Float. From here I glide to the surface.

I CAN DO WALL KICKS!

1.2.3.4.5.7. 8.9.10.

To Wall Kick, I hold onto the wall with my hands or float with just my fingertips pressing against the side of the pool. I let my legs extend out behind me and keep my arms straight with my elbows locked, to ensure I don't knock my head into the wall as I kick. I start slow and build up to kicking as fast and as hard as I can for 10 seconds at a time.

Flick your toes

BUTTERFLY

Butterfly Kick, which is also called Dolphin Kick, is like a wave that moves through my entire body. I start the wave by pressing my face into the water, keeping my arms just under the surface – the wave then flows from my chest pressing, hips rising, and feet flicking quickly up and down.

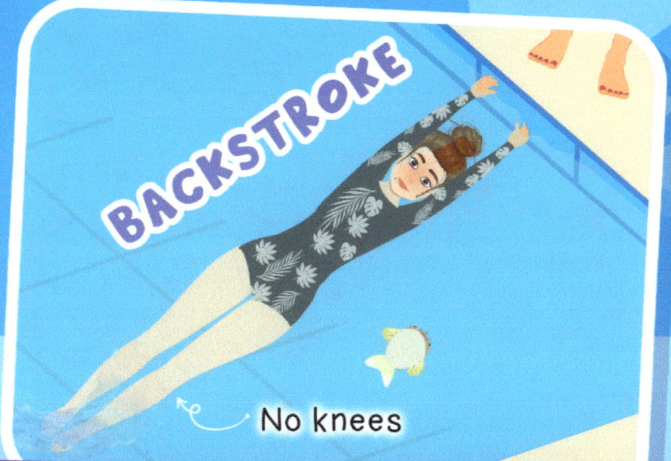

BACKSTROKE

No knees

For Backstroke Kick I focus on keeping my knees under the water as I use the soles of my feet and the back of my calves to press down on the water and kick it away. I let my toes just break the surface as I kick my feet back up, boiling the water and making lots of tiny bubbles.

BREASTSTROKE

Turn your Feet out

To Frog Kick for my Breaststroke, I make fast, little ankle circles with my heels by drawing my feet up behind me, turning them out, and swinging them around and together until my big toes touch. Before I restart each kick, I pause and count to 2 as I stretch and lift my feet so they are in line and hidden behind my body.

Fast little kicks

FREESTYLE

I practise Flutter Kick for my Freestyle by stretching out long with my legs close to the surface. I focus on keeping my feet floppy and ankles loose as they move up and down, creating lots of bubbles – not big splashes. As I kick, I turn my feet inwards so my big toes brush past each other with only my heels breaking the surface.

I CAN DO SIX KICKS PULL & BREATHE!

A constant and consistent kick as I swim Freestyle helps me maintain my balance when I turn to take a breath.

1.2.3.4.5.6! — Arms in line with shoulders — Fingertips down

I Blast Off from the wall and kick with both arms reaching forward and in line with my shoulders, just under the surface of the water. I tilt my wrists so my fingertips point slightly downwards. My eyes look at the bottom of the pool as I continue to kick and blow bubbles, counting to six in my head.

Press your ear — Push — **PULL & BREATHE!**

After 6 kicks, I lock one arm into place by pretending to glue it to the side of my head. This is my lead arm, it remains reaching forward as my breathing arm, also called my pulling arm, bends into a Power Triangle and pushes the water behind me all the way to the side of my leg. As my pulling arm passes through the water, I turn my head to the side and press my ear into the water to take a quick noisy Belly Breath.

When the hand of my pulling arm brushes past my leg, it is time to return my face back into the water. I roll onto my front as my arm arches over and my hand pierces the water, fingertips first. I kick 6 more kicks with both arms extended out front before turning to pull and breathe again

1.2.3.4.5.6! — Fingertips first

I challenge myself by breathing every 3 strokes, or by swapping my breathing arm and lead arm so I can practise breathing to the other side.

If I need help to count and balance on my lead arm, I can rest my hands on an adult's outstretched hands as they walk backwards and count with me.

I CAN FLY SKATE!

A Fly Skate teaches me to use my Power Triangles and when to breathe as I swim Butterfly.

Pull to the belly & out to the thigh

POWER TRIANGLES

To Fly Skate, I start in a Fly Float with my thumbs turned down and arms straight out in front of me. I do one slow Body Dolphin as I reach forward and bend my arms towards the bottom of the pool into Power Triangles. I use my Power Triangles to pull myself toward the surface and drive my face and shoulders up and out of the water.

Chin skim

I do 3 slow Body Dolphins under the water as I draw my hands back under me to return to my Fly Float.

As I skate over the water, my hands continue to push towards my belly button then all the way back to my thighs. I extend my chin forward, and skim over the surface, looking straight ahead to take in a quick Belly Breath. I then tuck my chin and look straight down as I return my face to the water.

I CAN DO A COBRA STRIKE!

> A Cobra Strike gives power and speed to my Breaststroke and helps me to time my breath correctly.

Cobra Strike

Power Triangles

Push

Find your toes

Turn your feet out

To Cobra Strike, I Blast Off from the wall using a Missile Start. I stay in the Missile Float with my thumbs touching as I do two slow Breaststroke kicks. As I kick, my face stays between my outstretched arms with my eyes looking down at the bottom of the pool. I reach as far forward as I can by pressing my armpits into the water. After I finish my second kick it is time to add my Cobra Strike.

To prepare for my Cobra Strike, I open the water in front of me by turning my thumbs down and catching the water with my hands, like I'm opening a set of curtains with my fingers. I then pull my head and shoulders up and out of the water by bending my elbows into Power Triangles and pushing the water towards my chest.

As I rise upwards, I look straight ahead, take in a quick breath and lean back. I also begin to draw my heels up behind me. This is my Cobra Strike position – my body is coiled and ready to strike.

As my head dives, face first, into the water between my outstretched arms, I stretch and glide just under the surface into a Missile Float and do two more Breaststroke kicks.

I CAN DO A BACKSTROKE RAINBOW!

A Backstroke Rainbow teaches me how to take off backwards, arching my body over the water, when I want to swim Backstroke.

THROW!

1. I hold onto the side of the pool with my arms shoulder-width apart. I then press my feet against the wall, and tuck my knees under my armpits, looking straight ahead.

2. I Blast Off by tilting my head back until I see the water behind me. I throw my arms backwards over my head like I do when I perform an Underwater Tumble on my back. I use the power in my legs and the soles of my feet to explode off the wall, making a Backstroke Rainbow arch with my entire body.

3. My hands and arms move into a Hyperstreamline, cutting through the water as I point my toes and kick my legs up to stop them from dragging over the surface

Once I am in the water, I whip my legs up and down as I Body Dolphin in my Hyperstreamline to the surface.

I CAN DO A SNOWBALL TURN!

To Snowball, I Blast Off from the wall and kick, face down in the water with my arms by my sides. When I am far enough away from the wall I do one small Dolphin Kick and perform an Underwater Tumble, landing on my back.

Snowballs teach me to change direction when I am swimming. I practise them slowly so I can learn to control how I land while not getting dizzy or disorientated.

Palms up

Torpedo Stretch

Tuck & spin

I make sure to tuck my chin and not lift my head before I flip. As I tumble, I draw my knees up to my chest and blow lots of Dragon Bubbles to stop water from going up my nose. When my feet break the surface I straighten and stretch out into a Hyperstreamline and look up at the sky.

When I can successfully perform a Snowball in the middle of the pool, I begin to move closer to the pool wall. I keep a safe distance so only my feet touch the wall. I am careful not to hit my head or hurt my legs as I turn.

If I am going to Snowball and change directions to swim Backstroke, I land and stay on my back. If I am going to swim Freestyle, I land and perform a Rotisserie Roll to Hyperstreamline onto my front.

When I can Snowball and land my feet safely on the wall, I bend my knees and Blast Off in my Hyperstreamline followed by 3 Body Dolphins back to the surface.

I CAN DO BELLY BUTTON SWIVEL KICKS!

To Belly Button Swivel Kick, I kick and rotate my body from side to side using my shoulders, hips and belly button.

Dip my shoulder

Eyes to the sky

Swivel your hips

I Blast Off from the side of the pool on my back into a Canoe Float. I keep my arms glued to my sides and tighten the muscles in my belly and back by pointing my toes and keeping my legs long as I power up my kick.

My eyes continue looking up at the sky as I keep as straight as I can and rotate my whole body from side to side. I swivel and dip my shoulders and hips as I kick the water toward each side of the pool.

I kick six fast kicks on my left then swivel my belly button and kick six fast kicks on my right.

I CAN DO A CATCH & THROW!

CATCH!

THROW!

The Catch and Throw is a land drill for practising my Backstroke Power Triangles.

To Catch and Throw, I stand on the pool deck or in shallow water, anchoring my feet, placing my hands at my sides, and looking straight ahead. I slowly straight-arm lift one arm over my head, brushing past my ear and reaching as far back as I can with my pinky finger

Without moving my head, I swivel from my belly button as I follow my arm and bend it behind me, pausing as if I'd just caught a ball. As I swivel, my other shoulder pauses in front of my chin

I then pretend to throw the ball to my leg by turning my hand over as I swivel my belly button back to face the other side. My throwing hand then lands on my leg.

I change sides, teaching both arms to Catch and Throw before trying the sequence that uses both arms. I move slowly and think hard as one arm lifts while the other one throws.

I CAN DO BACKSTROKE FINGERTIP DRAG!

Backstroke Fingertip Drag also teaches me to use my Backstroke Power Triangles.

POWER TRIANGLES

I practise with both arms, taking turns to lift, reach, bend and push with my paddle, whilst I rotate from side to side kicking, keeping my head steady looking straight up at the sky.

Straight arm lift

Shoulder to the sky

Bend & push

Pinky first entry

I Blast Off from the wall on my back, looking straight up at the sky with my hands resting on my thighs. I keep my kick strong and head steady as I lift one arm, swivel onto my side and reach as far back as I can with my pinky finger. Once my hand catches the water I begin to bend my arm behind me into a Power Triangle, keeping my hand and forearm upright and firm, like a paddle, with my fingertips poking through the surface of the water.

I push the water with my Power Triangle paddle all the way to my leg letting the water flow through my fingers as they drag through the water. When my hand passes my belly button I turn my hand over and flatten it, palm down, with my thumb touching my thigh. I then start again, with the other arm.

I CAN SWIM BUTTERFLY!

To practise and improve my Butterfly I swim Butterfly Walk Backs.

To do a Walk Back, I swim a short distance and then Push Out of the water to walk back to where I started. As I walk back to my starting point I can think about my swim – the parts of my stroke I got right and what I need to work on.

To swim Butterfly, I do a Swordfish Start and Hyperstreamline off the wall with 3 fast underwater Dolphin Kicks. When I reach the surface, I keep my eyes down and chin tucked as I separate my hands, keeping them firm as I angle my thumbs down to catch the water. I start my Butterfly Pull by bending my arms into Power Triangles, keeping my elbows high to pull myself forward.

The force of my Power Triangles moving under me help me rise out of the water, chin first, with eyes looking directly ahead as I take a quick breath. My arms extend all the way back as my thumbs graze past my thighs and I do one strong Dolphin Kick to help bring my arms out of the water.

Eyes down

Eyes forward

My arms swing around and recover over the water as I tuck my chin to my chest and throw my face under before my hands re-enter, thumbs first with palms down. As I land, I look straight down and do a second Dolphin Kick, pressing my chest into the water before I start the cycle again.

I start each Walk Back slow, and as I improve, I swim a bit faster and a bit further until I can swim Butterfly continuously for 1 minute.

I CAN SWIM BACKSTROKE!

For a Backstroke Walk Back, I do a Backstroke Rainbow Start and Hyperstreamline followed by 3 fast underwater Dolphin Kicks. When I reach the surface, I power up my kick and separate my hands, keeping one arm locked beside my ear. My head is steady as I look straight up and rotate to my side by dipping the shoulder of my moving arm into the water. I reach behind me with my pinky and catch the water with my firm hand.

If I want, I can have an adult count and tell me how many strokes I have before I reach the wall.

POWER TRIANGLES

Belly button swivel

Fast little kicks

Thumb to thigh

Pinky 1st Entry

I create a paddle with my arm by bending my elbow and using my Power Triangle to pull my body through the water. I swivel my hips, as fast as I can, out of the way as my hand turns over and pushes the water to my side. When my hand brushes my thigh and starts to lift, my other arm begins to reach and catch.

I breathe in and breathe out as my arms move fast to lift and drive my hands through the water. I stop before I reach the end of the pool so I don't bump my head.

I start each Walk Back slow, and as I improve, I swim a bit faster and a bit further until I can swim Backstroke continuously for 2 minutes.

I CAN SWIM BREASTSTROKE

For a Breaststroke Walk Back, I do an underwater Missile Start from the wall followed by one Breaststroke Kick. I keep my toes together and pointed behind me as I reach the surface and separate my hands, keeping them firm and turning my thumbs down slightly to catch the water.

POWER TRIANGLES

Insweep

Outsweep

Stretch & lift

Open the curtains

I start each Walk Back slow, and as I improve, I swim a bit faster and a bit further until I can swim Breaststroke continuously for 2 minutes.

I sweep my arms outwards as I bend my elbows and pull my body forward into my Power Triangles. I look straight ahead, and as I begin to rise my arms change direction to sweep inwards, towards each other to push the water to my chest.

I lift my head, chest and shoulders out of the water to take a quick breath, arching backward, before I Cobra Strike my body forward.

I drive myself back into the water, face first, as I shoot my hands over the surface and complete one fast Breaststroke Kick, squeezing the water between my legs and kicking it away with the soles of my feet. I glide in my Missile Float as my toes find each other and I begin the cycle again.

I CAN SWIM FREESTYLE

For a Freestyle Walk Back, I do a Swordfish Start and Hyperstreamline off the wall with 3 fast underwater Dolphin Kicks. When I reach the surface, I separate my hands until my arms are in line with my shoulders. I turn away from my lead arm as it reaches forward and I begin to catch the water with the hand of my pulling arm.

I bend my pulling arm under the water as I rock to my side and pull myself into the breathing position using my Power Triangle. I take a quick breath, pressing my ear into the water and keeping it close to my lead arm; meanwhile, my pulling arm pushes the water all the way back to the side of my leg.

POWER TRIANGLES

I start each Walk Back slow, and as improve, I swim a bit faster and a bit further until I can swim Freestyle continuously for 2 minutes

Lead arm stretch

Pinky 1st exit

As my pulling arm comes out of the water, I turn my hand towards my thigh so my pinky can exit first. I relax my hand as I raise my elbow and swing my arm over the surface of the water using my shoulders. I make sure to turn my face back into the water before my arm passes my head.

My lead arm begins to catch the water when my pulling arm finishes its journey to my leg. My lead arm then becomes my pulling arm as my other arm travels forward and enters the water.

Each arm enters fingertips first, like I'm reaching forward and slipping my hand into a long glove. I reach and rotate forward, Bubbling and Breathing, keeping my kick strong as I rock from side to side.

I CAN DO SIDE STROKE!

Side Stroke is a survival stroke used to conserve energy. It can be used to assist other swimmers or drag items back to a safe place. It looks and feels a lot like doing Breaststroke on your side.

PULL

To practise Side Stroke, I push off on my side with my lead arm reaching forward out front with my palm facing the bottom of the pool. I lay my ear and cheek on the water, like I am resting on a pillow, and look straight across the surface of the water. I keep my toes pointed and my other arm, also known as the trailing arm, against my side.

REACH

To move through the water, I draw my legs up behind me, by bending my knees, and push the water away with the soles of my feet. As my legs and feet are flexing and pushing, I bend and scoop the water with both arms. I pull the water under me with my lead arm and push the water away to my thigh with my trailing arm.

I try to sync up the reaching forward with my lead arm with the extending and stretching of my legs so I can glide in a line on my side through the water.

GLIDE

Once I can Side Stroke comfortably on my side, I challenge myself to Side Stroking using only my lead arm to propel me along. I keep my trailing arm at my side, resting on my thigh as I drag a kickboard, a rope or a pool noodle. This will help me learn to tow items through the water.

I CAN DIVE!

Before practising my Dive, I move to deeper water – but always with an adult who can swim. I check the depth, look for other people or submerged objects and check the signs around the pool before I dive in.

I stand on the edge of the pool and bend my knees slightly, locking my arms into a Hyperstreamline. My knees act as a wound up spring for when I push off with my feet and dive in.

I lock my hands and pretend to glue my arms to the sides of my head. It's important my arms and hands stay locked as I lean forward and point my fingertips to where I want to land in the water. If my head becomes unglued from my locked arms or my eyes look upwards instead of straight down when I dive in, I will belly flop and water will go up my nose. Squeezing the back of my head with my arms will help keep my arms in place and remind me to keep my eyes down.

Feet together

Eyes down

⚠ WARNING
SHUT THE GATE

1.6 m

When I am ready to Dive, I take in a deep Belly Breath, look down and hum. Leaning forward, I spring out from the side of the pool using my toes and the balls of my feet.

I arch my body over the water and follow my hands as I straighten my legs out behind me, pointing my toes. Once under the water, I maintain my speed by Hyperstreamlining and Dolphin Kicking to the surface.

I CAN DO A SURVIVAL SEQUENCE

A Survival Sequence can be lots of fun to practice, it also challenges my water safety knowledge and abilities.

To practise my Survival Sequence, I first move to deep water with an adult. Before I hop in, I use my thinking skills to answer a series of water safety questions, testing what I have learnt:

- Where is there a safe place to enter and exit the water?
- What is the emergency services phone number?
- What items around the pool can I grab to use for a reach rescue?
- What are our rules for water safety at home and around water?
- What is the number one rule for adults when children are playing in and around water?

1  **SAFE ENTRY** — 1.6 m

To start the Survival Sequence, I choose a safe entry or safety jump and enter the pool.

2 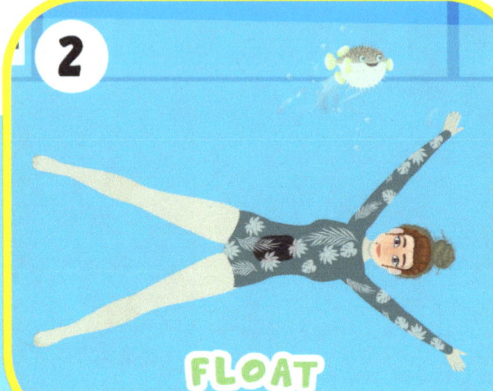 **FLOAT**

As I come up for air, I lay on my back and float for 1 or 2 minutes.

3  **CALL FOR HELP**

Next, I pretend to signal and call for help as I tread water for another minute or two.

4  **SWIM TO SAFETY**

Without putting my feet on the bottom of the pool or holding onto the sides, I swim to the end of the pool and Push-Out to safety.

It's best to swim using a stroke that doesn't use a lot of energy such as: – Side Stroke, Survival Backstroke or Breaststroke.

MY ACHIEVEMENTS CHECKLIST

1 I get a little bit better each time I practise my swimming skills.

2 I record my progress using the checklist and a pencil.

3 It reminds me which skills I am really good at and which skills I will need to practise.

4 I know the more I practice the better I will get.

5 When I have practiced and perfected every skill, I know I am ready to join a swim squad.

	Needs Work	Almost	Perfect
I can do a step-in & push-out			
I can belly breathe & sink down			
I can make power triangles			
I can hyperstreamline			
I can do a missile start			
I can do wall kicks			
I can do six kicks pull & breathe			
I can fly skate			
I can do a cobra strike			
I can do a backstroke rainbow			
I can do a snowball turn			
I can do belly button swivel kicks			
I can do a catch & throw			
I can do backstroke fingertip drag			
I can swim butterfly			
I can swim backstroke			
I can swim breaststroke			
I can swim freestyle			
I can do side stroke			
I can dive			
I can do a survival sequence			

www.ingramcontent.com/pod-product-compliance
Lightning Source LLC
Chambersburg PA
CBHW050853010526
44107CB00047BA/1599